TASTES LIKE CHICKEN

Travel Tales & Tidbits

by

Cedric Brown

Tastes Like Chicken

© 2025

ISBN: 978-0-9857006-7-6

All rights reserved

Most names of private citizens mentioned in the essays have been changed.

None of this work was generated by Artificial Intelligence.

for my dear mother
Carolyn A.
who always cares about where i've been
what i've seen
& which adventures i've had

PREFACE

My first exposure to wanderlust came through legendary poet and writer, Langston Hughes, an early favorite author of mine. His memoirs, *The Big Sea* and *I Wonder as I Wander*, are captivating catalogues of a true citizen of the world. His travel tales become even more amazing considering their early twentieth century social context, starring Mr. Hughes as a Black man moving about the globe without fear, wherever opportunity and cargo ships took him.

Before my own travels abroad became a priority and regular occurrence, I held a simmering envy of people who, like Mr. Hughes, roamed the world, point to point, free from day-to-day weight of routines and ruts. Their lives seemed full of thrills and adventures. But I usually ended up wondering as they wandered, *What are they looking for?* People have asked the same of me in my pursuits to travel far over land and sea.

I am very fortunate to have had the resources, opportunities, and agency to follow my lifelong yearning to travel. And at moments while writing I thought this collection of stories—all true—would sound like so much humblebragging, I also felt an obligation to share what I have gathered from travels across the world.

I share because Black Americans need to see and understand ourselves outside of the stereotypes that still constrain our images inside U.S. borders.

I share because LGBTQ perspectives in the face of a too-often hostile world still serve to validate our everyday existence.

I share because I believe that, at the end of the day, our common humanity enables us to relate to any story of challenge or change, regardless of the identity of the storyteller.

Since I am a poet at heart, I am thankful for the growing popularity of flash and micro writing. I hope you will enjoy these micro essays, meant to provide a toe-dip but not a deep end plunge into these travel experiences, a firsthand testimony that good people, good times, and good lessons in living exist nearly everywhere. Someday I may write more.

By the way, these essays are not in any chronological order.

Best wishes on your reading journey, and as my Irish friends might say, "May the road rise up to meet you."

Cedric Brown
Winston-Salem, North Carolina, USA
August 2025

ONE

ZIMBABWE
On the Edge

WHY *did I not think to change currency* before *leaving Cape Town?* I wondered, fidgeting. I figured I could stroll by an ATM while in the Victoria Falls airport as I usually do elsewhere, withdrawing cash at a reasonable exchange rate.

But there I was, in the immigration line, needing to pay for an entry visa. In the immigration line with no cash. In Zimbabwe. With. No. Cash. Robert Mugabe, the notorious freedom fighter-turned-demagogue, was in the final months of his dictator-like presidency. His photo portrait hung with care in the otherwise austere arrivals hall, glaring out over queuing visitors.

My hands started to sweat. *Dang, how am I going to pay? Will they make me go back to South Africa? Will they detain me? Will I need to bribe someone?* How I'd bribe someone while carrying no cash made little to no sense, but logic under pressure isn't always my friend. I craned my neck, looking around for an ATM, but was also aware that if I looked too fidgety, security might pull me from the line, which was especially scary given Mugabe's frequent antigay rages. He had once called us "worse than pigs and dogs."

Oh snap. I was next in the queue. I stepped up to the kiosk and handed my passport to the officer, deciding to appeal to his mercy. "Sir, I don't have any hard currency. If someone could escort me to a nearby automatic teller, I could…"

He cut me off with a gentle raised hand. "Sir, no worries. Do you have a credit card?" he replied, pulling out a portable credit card reader, the kind frequently used overseas but not in the States. Whewwww! Saved!

Transaction completed, he stamped my passport and waved me through. "Welcome to Zimbabwe, and enjoy your visit."

The next day, after a first time sleeping underneath a mosquito net, I ambled awestruck through the fine spray and nonstop roar generated by the world's largest waterfall, Victoria Falls. Mosi-ao-Tunya, its indigenous name meaning "the smoke that thunders," well captures its essence. Rainbows spring from the chasm twenty-five meters wide and one hundred meters deep. The volume of water from the Zambezi River hurling over the cliff is breathtaking–an average of a million gallons per second!

On the other side of the chasm, opposite the river, I wandered down the tree-lined, sometimes slippery stone path from viewpoint to viewpoint, watching the cascade in action. The misty air made for a magical, almost mystical experience here at the meeting of borders, Zimbabwe and Zambia. A spirit of tremendous fortune washed over me— you're standing in Africa–Africa! The Motherland of legends and ancestors' dreams! Of *Jet* covers and *Ebony* features! A childhood wish come true! The negative ions of the moist air, the natural result of evaporating water, made me feel giddy with awe and glee. Or maybe it was something bigger.

This is one of the best things I've ever done, I thought. So worth the price of admission, sweaty palms and all.

TWO

GREECE
The Old Man & The Sea

My first visit to Greece brought back two memories from childhood, ones that had no direct links to the popular and revered tourist destination but hinted at everyday commonality.

One of my first stops as a tourist was the Panathenaic Stadium, the restored arena where the first Olympic Games of the modern era were held upon their revival in 1896, after a nearly 2,000 year hiatus. As a kid, I was a superfan of the Olympics. I could rattle off all the host cities of the modern summer games in chronological order. I dreamt of duplicating the great Jesse Owens' feat of winning four gold medals, until puberty and my genetics put an end to those dreams. (Although sometimes I still fantasize about it!)

There in Athens, I roamed in wonder through steep rows of seating carved entirely from marble, admiring the impressive symmetry and order. Other tourists meandered through the stadium, also imagining themselves as spectators to ancient athletic glory. I sent a grinning selfie to my sisters and brothers; having witnessed my boyhood obsession with Olympic history, only they would understand how geeked out I was at that moment!

Days later, after the excitement of a week-long conference in the capital, retreating to the rocky countryside across the cobalt blue Myrtoan Sea was a welcome relief. Ermioni, a small seaside town of 5,000 people, offered a calm respite after the stress and fast pace of Athens.

Our lodge clerk recommended taking a meal at a nearby tavern with outdoor seating, a fine walk past Ermioni's main pier, a half dozen other restaurants, and over a small hill dotted with quiet stone houses of bleached white walls. True to the clerk's instructions, the tavern sat on a narrow lane hugging a short cliff, buffeted by a very blue sea.

Hubby and I sat, two of us at a table for four, overlooking that very blue sea, where loud and lanky teenagers executed energetic dives off the cliff. I was proud of myself for sounding out the Greek-lettered menu items, having memorized the Greek alphabet as a college undergraduate hellbent on joining a Greek-lettered fraternity. That trivia finally came in handy beyond swiftly passed college days.

We ordered and received golden zucchini fritters with a cloud-light side of tzatziki, and fava (yellow split peas) that came accompanied by a scary-sized mound of zingy chopped red onions. I'd also decided to try the sardines, spurred by a hazy association with my grandfather.

Papa Charlie, my mama's daddy, was a quiet, half-smiling man, slow-moving with age, who commanded a great respect from those who encountered him as the family sage and great provider. I remember him eating sardines from a tin can at the Formica kitchen table, likely alongside saltine crackers and cucumber slices doused in vinegar and black pepper. Decades later and thousands of miles away, nudged by that faint image, I was tempted to try sardines anew, presumably plucked fresh from the very blue sea.

The quartet of fish arrived at our table, plated as a stack of beautiful silver slivers, giants at about five inches each, and headless in a vinegary olive oil marinade. They were tangy and delicious, fishy and intense on the tongue. I'm usually not a fan of raw fish consumed as sushi or ceviche, but these sardines fit the bill that day. I wolfed down the whole plate of them, throwing intimidating looks through slitted eyes at two cats crouching nearby.

Upon returning Stateside, I made a beeline for my favorite posh grocery store to buy tinned sardines in various marinades. This sensory souvenir took me back to the sense of contentment and relaxation in the summer heat. A kind of tasty delight my grandfather already knew.

THREE

BRAZIL
Last Night the Samba Saved My Life

Samba saved my life. Not that my life was ever in any real danger, but samba—the Brazilian music and dance—came into my life, jerked me forward, and flung me into years of fun.

Bored and saddened by a still-raw relationship breakup, I accepted an invitation to join a friend at a dance class fitness workout (years before the Zumba craze). On balance, I'm a good dancer—great at freestyling, not so great with following choreography. I've always loved expressing myself through lively movement; I believe dance is the celebratory spirit of life itself.

I accepted the invitation, went to this class, and was turned *out* by the live percussion—several different types of drums that rode on the rhythm established by the big bass drum, the surdo, which means "deaf" in Portuguese. And deafening it was!

My favorite percussive instrument is no doubt the cuica, a type of drum that is rubbed rather than pounded, the friction making a sound well described as an itch. And that's the most, ahem, *polite* way to describe it!

It was impossible to stay still in class, as we moved barefoot across the floor in waves with other students, following the lead of the charismatic dance instructor, Rhonda, who was tall and taut-muscled with a blond ponytail and joyous vibe.

Samba—not the pointy-toed ballroom type but the funkier original version by regular folk—isn't explained with ease. It's kind of a three step to a four count beat; it's feet front and back and knees side to side; it's hips shaking while the head and shoulders stay still. It's crazy!

I loved samba, the dance and the music, and became pretty good at it, for a non-native. I followed a local samba band around San Francisco as they gigged in different places, always stepping and shouldering my way into the front line of dancers near the stage. Some of the musicians didn't like my presence—this Black, queer man shimmying and shaking with the ladies—but I didn't care. I would often dance into soreness and dehydration, but the satisfaction was worth it. Plus it was a good way to channel unspent sexual energy between too-infrequent hookups.

During those lean dollar days, I decided to treat myself to a trip to Brazil, mostly to sample samba in its birthplace. I was well inspired by the tales of journalist and MacArthur Fellow, Alma Guillermoprieto, in *Samba*. The small book is a fascinating ethnographic account of her immersion in a Rio de Janeiro favela community as it prepared for the world's most celebrated Carnaval.

Samba has evolved from its outlawed origins in the steep hillside settlements of Brazil's formerly enslaved Africans, the last in the Western Hemisphere to be freed from bondage in 1888. While now part of the national heritage, samba still strongly carries its African Bantu roots in its complex polyrhythms and cultural protocols.

Once I was on the ground after the sixteen-hour journey from the U.S., I strolled around open-mouthed as I stared at the iconic sights of Copacabana and Ipanema beaches. My guide, an English-speaking friend of a friend, agreed to help me get to one of the samba schools, the associations that organize contingents for the Carnival parade and competition. But we were limited in where we could go, due to the volatile rainy season and compromised safety for non-residents, since some of these schools were located in tough communities.

On my last night in Rio, we traveled to Salgueiro, one of the top ten samba schools in Rio, to join their revelry. We arrived by cab at the open air gymnasium-type dance hall, decorated in the school's signature colors of red and white. The sound of the bateria—the nearly one hundred-strong drumming corps—was like thunder; it seized my legs and whipped me into dancing. I marveled at the intricate steps and whirls of the school's flag-bearer and dance master, the leaders of the troupe.

From the packed dance floor, folks sang full-throated along with the lyrics booming from the live band. This was just an early rehearsal, I learned. Over the next months, the dancing would become more organized and costumed in preparation for the next Carnival competition, where Salgueiro ultimately placed fifth.

By the evening's end, in the wee hours of the morning, I was completely soaked in my own sweat. It was one of those rare moments where I felt that if I dropped dead right there, I would've entered the afterlife sore and dehydrated, but with no regrets.

Samba—the music and the dance—will always beat in syncopation with the rhythm of my own heart.

FOUR

UNITED ARAB EMIRATES
What Lies Underneath

I don't remember ever hearing about Dubai prior to the year 2000. By pouring huge sums into the city's transformation, the Emiratis have crafted their second city–only the capital, Abu Dhabi, is larger–into a must-see exotic destination for luxury-seeking travelers from across the globe. Dubai isn't the place for eco-tourism or a pious pilgrimage; people visit Dubai for its ultra-high-end offerings–pampering, dining, shopping, adventure-seeking. It's a gleaming, fancy playground, Las Vegas on steroids but without the gambling and legalized sex trade.

At least those were my impressions. I'd scheduled a nine hour layover while passing through DXB, their sparkling airport packed with amenities and the connecting hub for the best long-haul aviation experiences I've ever had.

Arriving about an hour after sundown, I was waved through Emirati immigration by stern officers in crisp epaulettes, bearded and unsmiling. The night air was so hot—99°F / 37°C—that condensation dripped from the windows inside the beautiful bright glass and steel terminal. I'd arranged a four-hour city tour and was met curbside in the arid heat of the airport arrivals zone by the friendly young Egyptian, Arif, who was to be my guide.

Arif and I set off in his Lexus SUV, zooming around the still-searing and still-bustling city. He was an enthusiastic advocate for his new homeland, very proud of its development, and knowledgeable about the different points of interest he showed me.

I was struck by how shiny and new everything seemed, as though these architectural marvels had sprung shimmering from the desert dunes one evening.

Dubai is a study in fabulosity. The Burj Al Arab: the dhow-shaped hotel reputed to offer seven-star luxury! The Palm Jumeirah: the man-made island archipelago clustered offshore in the shape of a palm tree! The Burj Khalifa: the world's tallest building, a tiered spire reaching into the heavens while an evening light show synced with dancing water fountains at the base of the building!

In the midst of all this modernity, my favorite moment was much simpler. Arif and I boarded an abra, a small wooden ferry, and zipped across Dubai Creek in ten minutes to the Old City, where we visited the Spice Souk, a longtime source of mercantile wealth for area traders. Alongside the mounds and bins of great varieties of spices in this market—curries and cinnamons, cardamoms and cloves, among others—sat beautiful displays of saffron. The tiny red tubules of brilliant scarlet lay on display in intricate gold and crystal chalices shelved in glass showcases. Saffron, the dried stamen of a particular species of crocus flower, is the world's most expensive spice, averaging upwards of $250 per pound. I purchased a small amount, a literal pinch, as a keepsake.

As we left the spice market, retracing our way back to the car, the last of the day's calls to prayer sounded from the nearest minaret, resounding into the dry night. The scene felt ancient and a bit otherworldly. Pausing in the streets as the serpentine notes of the Adhan hung in the air, I appreciated witnessing this tradition, older and deeper than the pylons sunk into the desert to support the many flashy skyscrapers. I valued this sobering reminder of the foundation, nearly two thousand years old, on which the gleaming urban playground stands.

FIVE

AUSTRALIA
'Cos We're Free

'Cos I'm freeeee
Because I'm free

This is a magical story from a different Oz, unrelated to the Wizard but maybe more powerful. This is a tale of two incredible indigenous Australian women, contemporaries who've shared a spotlight and a song in front of their nation and the world.

I first noticed Catherine Freeman when, as a teenager, she represented her native Australia in the 1992 Barcelona Olympics in the 400-meter run. As the television broadcasters introduced the athletes in that race, one announcer referred to Cathy's desire to become a lawyer working on behalf of Aboriginal rights. That kind of political identification and aspiration caught my attention. Who was this slender brown woman from a nation often thought of as mostly blonde?

As I came to learn, many Australian Aboriginal people call themselves "Black," both as a descriptor of darker complexions and of political identity. Like their Black and Native American counterparts, they have been challenged throughout history by colonization, intense racism, and oppressive discrimination from white citizens.

A few years after that TV introduction to Cathy Freeman, I visited friends in Sydney, where I set out to learn more about the self-described Black folks in this corner of the world.

One evening while Down Under, my friends and I attended a town hall concert of a young singer-songwriter on the rise, Christine Anu. Christine is a Torres Strait Islander, a large community of indigenous people from the archipelago of islands just north of Queensland province. At the time of the concert, Christine had just released her debut album, *Stylin' Up*, which incorporated themes of identity, coming-of-age, and societal expectations with humor, yearning, and sass. The concert that night was a bit demure, as Christine was only accompanied by a sole guitarist. As talented as they both were, the crowd remained polite and reserved, clapping thoughtfully from their seats.

A week later, we saw Christine again, this time with a full band in front of a younger, vibrant, and loudly appreciative crowd in her hometown of Cairns. I bought Stylin' Up home as a souvenir and came to love it, both the music and as a reminder of a splendid trip to Oz.

After her Olympic debut, Cathy went on to greater glory, first becoming a double gold medalist at the 1994 Commonwealth Games, winning the 200 and 400 meters. There, to the consternation of some, she carried both the Australian and Aboriginal flags on her victory laps around the track. On the world stage, she ran to a brilliant silver medal in the 400 meters at the 1996 Olympics in Atlanta, setting her personal best and one of the top twenty fastest times ever in that event. She also earned dual world championships (1997 and 1999) in the 400 meters.

While she was already a national superhero, her crowning achievement was without a doubt her clear victory at the 2000 Olympics in Sydney, in front of the largest crowd ever assembled for an athletics meet, a whopping 112,000 fans. This, only days after she had the rarefied honor of lighting the Olympic cauldron in the opening ceremony of the games.

Bearing the enormous hopes and expectations of the home crowd, at that moment Cathy was the most visible and revered indigenous woman–or person of any stripe–in Australia.

Christine Anu also had a stellar year in 2000, singing her signature "My Island Home" in the Olympic closing ceremony, seeing her debut album reach platinum status, and releasing her second album, *Come My Way*. That sophomore collection featured the crescendoing, soaring, chorus-backed "'Cos I'm Free," a tribute to her compatriot Cathy Freeman, based on the tattoo inscription on the athlete's right shoulder. "'Cos I'm Free" became an anthem of empowerment and a glorious reminder to strive for authenticity every day.

These sisters from Oz inspire me with their talent, soul, and uncompromised connections to home and heritage. Signifying freedom with a voice ringing through the wind, or running propelled by it.

SIX

GHANA
Wrapped in Glory

My first trip to the Motherland took me to Ghana, land of the Black Star. I've since told many others that Ghana is a wonderful gateway to West Africa for American descendants of the enslaved. The widespread use of English, its compact size, and welcoming people make it manageable. The lush, gorgeous flora evokes the Caribbean and the U.S. South; a clear and direct line to the African experience in the Americas is rooted in the colonial forts along the Atlantic Coast and the kente cloth tradition.

Two of the best-known coastal forts, Elmina and Cape Coast Castle, are UNESCO World Heritage sites. These dungeons held kidnapped Africans before they were shipped as cargo across the Atlantic in the Middle Passage. These sites of forced departure, with haunting Doors of No Return, are now places of redemption for descendants of the enslaved, returning to acknowledge ancestors in solemn reclamation rituals. The experience at the forts is unforgettable, a marker of a very low era in human history. Many shed tears; many tears are shed.

A road trip further upcountry, traveling through bright emerald forests and grassy hills of the Ashanti region, provides dazzling solace. An outgoing tour guide drove a friend and me from Accra to Kumasi, Ghana's second largest city. This five hour journey took us down two-lane roads that cut black ribbons across the rolling countryside, winding through tiny villages dotted with kids in bright uniforms marching to and from school. On occasion I closed my eyes to keep from screaming as our driver swung wide, racing to overtake and pass another vehicle, oncoming traffic in full view. Fortunately we arrived at our destination without a scratch.

Now for the dazzling part: kente, kente everywhere! The small village of Bonwire, a short drive from Kumasi, is the traditional home of the colorful, intricately woven cloth. Legend has it that two brothers created the first kente by watching a spider spin a web. Unsurprising lore in the land of Anansi, the legendary arachnid. Weavers sit surrounded by complex wooden contraptions, pedals beneath their feet, looms spread large in front of them, heddles and warps and wefts mixed in. It's like trying to understand what's in an airplane cockpit.

Kente has been adapted in North America as a widespread symbol of Black pride. The most recognizable patterns are black and gold stripes and zigzags, often interspersed with maroon or green thread. The weavers in Bonwire weren't limited to that four color palette; I saw shades and tones from pastel pinks and teals to bright royal purples and the occasional crisp whites. Some weavers even incorporated ink stamps of Ghanaian Adinkra symbols onto the broad swaths of cloth, each icon representing a principle, value, or story.

What an amazing sight, standing before walls of stacked kente, fresh from the loom, color combos and patterns without end, in shop after shop! Kente, kente everywhere! I wanted to purchase at least two to honor and support the master craftwork on display. It was hard to choose! Years later, I still have a gorgeous black, white, and gold kente that I only bring out on special occasions.

After being dazzled by kente in its birthplace, it became harder to swallow too-pervasive stereotypes of Africans as "primitive." Kente is but one sophisticated cultural tradition in a vast array of African riches. As our cultural inheritance, we get to show our great pride in embracing those riches, draping them across our backs, and wrapping ourselves in their glorious warmth.

SEVEN

BRITAIN
A History in Music

I learned about Black Brits through music. My coming-of-age cassette and compact disc collection included Loose Ends, Musical Youth, Billy Ocean, Incognito, Mica Paris, Brand New Heavies, and everything Sade ever released. I will also admit to a low-key crush on Mikey, the guitarist from Culture Club—chiiiile, those luscious arms! And when supergroup Soul II Soul's first hit crossed the pond, I learned how to do the Running Man by following the beat to "Keep on Movin'." 'Twas the beginning of a beautiful relationship.

It was also through music that I came to understand a landmark in Black British history. The title song of Caron Wheeler's first solo album, *UK Blak*, highlights the arrival of the first mass wave of Black immigrants. Named the Windrush Generation after the vessel that sailed from the British West Indies to the UK, the Caribbean migrants–understood to be subjects of the Crown–arrived in England at the invitation of the post-war government with big hopes of lucrative work, and essentially got stuck there, unable to afford returning to their home islands.

On my first visit to London, I bunked at a friend's boyfriend's place in South London, having swapped my little San Francisco studio apartment for his spacious Herne Hill home. (The generosity of queer social networks is worth mentioning here.) In setting out to take in the city, of course I wanted to see the neighborhood of Brixton as much as Big Ben and Buckingham Palace.

A longtime home to a large Afro-Caribbean community, Brixton was also the site of the legendary nightclub The Fridge, where Soul II Soul grew into an international phenomenon through a regular club night residency there. Brixton is also one stop north of Herne Hill on the Southeastern Railway, a commuter line, which made my pilgrimage easy.

When I stepped off the train and noticed the trashy environs of the train station next to the raised tracks, I muttered to myself, "Figures they have the Black people in the damn nasty dump." But rounding the corner onto Brixton Road, just in front of the Brixton Underground Station, was a revelation.

I ended up there just as a subway train had arrived and emptied, releasing a steady flow of passengers to stream up the stairs and into the streets. A funky bassline boomed from a kiosk situated just inside the station entrance, the perfect soundscape as a lean-limbed, shaved bald, beat-faced sista dressed in a natty long maxi vest—giving *Essence* chic—strode past me and melted into the larger crowd.

Energy, lights, sound, color. This. Was. Brixton.

I made my way further down the thoroughfare into the thick of things, ending up on the Electric Avenue of Eddy Grant's Grammy-nominated song of the same name. At the time, Electric Avenue and the adjacent covered markets were mostly shops and stalls for everyday shopping: fresh produce, dynamic Dutch wax print fabrics, electronics, household wares, and–as home to halal butchers–way too much raw meat for my taste!

I was fascinated by the comingling of ethnicities there, namely Africans and West Indians, with some Middle Easterners and South Asians in the mix, each contributing different attire, accents, languages, and energies to the bustling market scene.

Nowadays Brixton Market is a tamer, gentrified version of its former self, housing chichi eateries and artisan shoppes, but it's still a colorful and lively space, well worth the visit and still one of my favorite places in one of my favorite cities.

In a fitting full circle moment, on a return trip years later, I thoroughly enjoyed Soul II Soul's thirtieth anniversary concert at the London Palladium, where I sang along to allll the lyrics and stood dancing in place amidst the swirling theater lightshow.

At one point I looked around and thought, *Who are all these old people out on a school night?* Doh! This was *my* generation. People my same age—still young at heart, reliving good times through great tunes.

Jazzie B and crew put on an amazing, memorable performance with their exquisite musicianship and deep-seated one love vibe, still Afrocentric but welcoming everyone. As Jazzie B says, "A happy face, a thumpin' bass, for a loving race." Thank you, Brixton!

EIGHT

MEXICO
Birth of a Traveler

I took my first solo trip abroad at age fifteen as part of a planned school excursion to Mexico, with three stops on our itinerary: Mexico City, the mighty megalopolis; the little mountain town of Taxco, renowned for its silver trade; and coastal Acapulco, arguably in the last breaths of its 1970s chic heyday.

This certainly was a journey of discovery, my first

time traveling overseas without my family. Our group flew Eastern Airlines from Atlanta over the Gulf of Mexico, so I counted it as traveling "overseas." This wasn't my first time over an international border. As a younger kid, when my family visited relatives in Detroit, we drove southward through the Detroit-Windsor Tunnel and emerged in Canada, which was a thrill to end up "in a whole (n)other country!" But for me, at 15, the air travel to Mexico was next level.

I was amazed by Mexico City: its size and spectacle as the largest city in North America; the phenomenal history in its foundation, literally built on top of the ancient Aztec capital of Tenochtitlan; and the geographic wonder that it is at 7,000 feet above sea level. I still consider it a favorite destination.

I have vivid memories of climbing the pyramids of Teotihuacán, gawking at the huge stone relief of the Aztec sun calendar in the world-famous Museum of Anthropology, feeling overwhelmed in the huge Zócalo square in the center city, and attending a colorful evening performance of the Ballet Folklórico at the opulent Palacio de Bellas Artes.

A Diego Rivera masterpiece, *Dream of a Sunday Afternoon in Alameda Central,* captured my full attention. I was fascinated by that intricate and slightly sinister mural of historical figures on display in the vestibule of our hotel. The next time I visited Mexico City, nearly twenty years later, the hotel had been destroyed in the huge 1985 earthquake, but the mural had been recovered and moved to its own museum building, national treasure that it is.

Food is a powerful evocator of memory. Whenever I see a churro, the deep-fried crispy dough stick rolled in cinnamon and sugar, I think about Mexico City.

I was introduced to churros the night that our tour group attended the Ballet Folklórico performance. I dressed up, thinking I was suave while sporting a red knit tie and matching red and gray windbreaker with a popped collar. Our group gathered in a smallish cafe, preparing to chow down on churros and hot chocolate as is the custom (Mexico has a deep heritage around cacao). A cute young woman wearing bright pink lipstick approached me from a nearby table and asked for a kiss. When someone, maybe our tour guide, translated her request for me, I nodded wide-eyed with a surprised, *"¡sí!"* and stuck out my cheek. Her companions laughed and clapped, and she smiled. I wore that pink smudge on my cheek for the rest of the evening as a testament to my suaveness. I guess I was the hot chocolate to go along with her churro.

I consider this voyage as the occasion where I got my tacky tourist tics out of my system, notably an unfortunate streetside moment with a sombrero and maracas. Thank God there was no social media; I would've been cancelled without a doubt. All I'll say is that the trip highlighted the necessary art of subtlety and humility when visiting another country and culture. I have vowed never again to reinforce the garish Ugly American reputation that weighs us down like overstuffed backpacks. This trip also whet my appetite for learning more about how people live every day, their histories and expressions, how we're alike and different.

It was then and there that I became a traveler.

NINE

Thailand
Sacred Smile

Bangkok has canals?! Who knew? Built off and around the Chao Phraya River, which bisects the city, the canals connect the Thai capital's markets, homes, and sights in a fashion similar to its roadways—with way less traffic congestion!

Hubby and I rode in canoe-like motorized longtail boats during our river-based tour of the ever-moving city, stopping to lunch on scrumptious spicy hot curry entrees on a blisteringly hot day. Does eating hot food help the body stay cool? Maybe. I'm not convinced. But being on the water also seemed to help tame the heat exposure, at least a little!

Historic Bangkok features a skyline of striking golden-spired shrines and other sacred sites as tributes to their royal family as well as their Buddhist spiritual practices. My clear favorite was Wat Pho, the Temple of the Reclining Buddha. This was the first time I'd ever encountered a relaxed, contemplative, even joyful sacred figure at a site of worship.

Consider this: where are the depictions in Western iconography of Christ laughing? I bet he did, out of gratitude or delight. Human beings are funny. That's my point. Spirituality includes joy, not just monotonous piety.

Wat Pho spoke to me as a reminder that, "There is whimsy even in the sacred," as I later wrote in a poem. Half the size of a football field, the golden bronze

Buddha figure lies reclined on its right leg and arm, hand propped behind its head, as though looking up from a chaise longue, with a slight smile as if awakening from a peaceful, pleasing dream. That sight in turn made *me* smile.

I also appreciated the general air of calm, gratitude, and respect that I found on that first trip to Thailand, despite the intense heat and ever-present traffic.

Our tour guide, a friendly college student working part time, taught us a moderated form of the Thai greeting, the *wai*, a graceful bow of acknowledgement. The greeter presses their hands together flat palmed like the Western prayer gesture. Depending on the status of the person being greeted, the greeter will position the hands along an axis somewhere between the heart and the forehead—the higher up, the more reverence and deference the greeter shows. When greeting friends and peers, place hands at the chest level. For elders and seniors, press hands together at the chin, and salute holy figures with clasped hands to forehead. Each greeting is accompanied by a brief bow, again showing courtesy and deference: the lower one bows, the more respect is being paid.

As foreigners, we weren't obligated to use or return the greetings, but I loved the wai, and kept doing a basic version of it even after leaving Thailand. As with the Indian *namaste* and the Japanese *ojigi*, I think of bowing as a gracious show of respect and peace, less aggressive than a handshake and less intrusive than a hug (which are still legit forms of greetings). All such gestures point to our desire to connect with and "see" other people. And that's what travel elsewhere is all about: seeing and connecting, learning and respecting.

TEN

MOZAMBIQUE
Hold On to Your Dreams

Mozambique gets a bad rap, as it's often cited—when cited at all—as one of the world's poorest countries. But once I started to explore its capital, Maputo, I found a vibrant art scene in the crumbling but buzzing city. "Crumbling" in that, like Havana, many physical structures were in a state of disrepair well after the heyday of their architectural glory during colonization and occupation. And "buzzing" in that there was a palpable energy of people on the move, getting their side hustle up and running, hanging out their business shingle wherever possible—tents, stalls, abandoned storefronts, sidewalks, pop-up spaces, and so on.

I returned several times to the National Art Museum to view *Um Povo Unido* (*A United People*), a mind-blowing life-sized sculpture by Samussone Macamo. Its magic lay in its interlocking and elongated limbs and faces emerging from a single tall piece of sandalwood, a tree in human form (or human form in a tree). No cameras were allowed in the museum, but I did try my hand at sketching the incredible statue, to unsatisfactory result.

After lunch in an outdoor cafe alongside dapper short-sleeved businessmen conducting cool conversations on Bluetooth headsets, I popped into a gallery exhibition of works by a local artist, Carlos Fornasini. This amazing painter offers vibrant figurative works of women and birds accented by layers of tiny colored dots that collectively burst or saunter off the canvas.

All told, I visited five galleries and was wowed by the variety and quality of work on display. Who knew?

The most serendipitous moment in what was becoming a satisfying tour of African art came from a one-night jazz performance at the Franco-Mozambican Cultural Center.

Fighting my introvert's first instinct to stay in my room, I thought, *Jazz is universal and it'll give me something to do this eve, so why not?*

I'm so glad to have ventured out. Siya Makuzeni, the guest artist, was featured front and center with her band. A South African musical dynamo, Siya ruled the stage in her one-piece brown and gold jumpsuit that I remembered as leopard skin because she was a fierce and focused performer, wielding her trombone, nearly as tall as she was, like a third arm. Siya was a musician's musician—short on the stage patter, big on the musical output of her original improv-driven pieces. She punctuated the melodies with intricate staccato scatting and yielded the floor to her ensemble-mates for enthusiastic solos. But no one else in the band possessed her musical charisma. She was just dynamite!

I downloaded her new album, most of which was original material that the band covered in the show. Three favorites, all of which came with upbeat lyrics of encouragement, include "Hold On", "New Age", and "Moya Oyingcwele," an isiXhosa praise and prayer to ancestors. The entire album, *Out of This World*, became my soundtrack for unforgettable travels in southern Africa that year.

I had the added pleasure of seeing Siya again when she brought her unflagging energy to Los Angeles two years later, and enjoyed her just as much.

Maputo was a pleasant surprise, poverty notwithstanding, and I noted in my journal that the city emanated a feeling that their worst days were behind them after a brutal fifteen-year civil war from 1977 to 1992. I hope so. Perhaps I was just witnessing everyday business of everyday people, but I sensed something more—a renaissance, as the artistic energy conveyed a blossoming and flourishing culture that counters its media soundbite reputation as a locus of despair. As I saw and heard with my own eyes and ears, one truly can't always judge a book by its cover.

ELEVEN

France
Pied-à-Terre

Ah, Gay Paree. While not known for a freewheeling gay men's social scene like Amsterdam, Berlin, and now Madrid, Paris is . . . well, Paris! The capital of romance and allure! But experiencing queer Parisian nightlife wasn't easy for a broken-French-speaking reluctant clubgoer like me. I can handle my business on the dance floor, but I'm clueless at the bar, where I can barely hear anything over pounding techno music and shouted conversations, let alone carry on a charming conversation in another tongue. And yet, I persist.

In Paris I checked out a hotspot with mostly African and Caribbean cuties who, like their U.S. counterparts, squealed and flooded the dance floor when Queen Bey came throbbing through the speakers. That spot was fun, with great eye candy, but no connection.

I went to the legendary tea dance, Blac, Blanc, Beur (Black, White, Arab) to experience that particular tricolor French ethnic mix. Again, it offered nice eye candy and so-so music, but I was left with the impression that, for a reluctant clubgoer like me, a club is a club is a club, regardless of location. I'm much better off in small group conversation in a reasonably lit room filled with some kinda groove humming in the background. But I digress.

One evening I decided to try my luck in Le Marais, Paris' renowned gay district in the center city's 4th

Arrondissement. By "luck," I meant attempting to have an entertaining conversation and share spirits with a bilingual hometown crowd. I wasn't explicitly looking to get laid, but I guess my aura said otherwise. Before I knew it, I was chatting with a Swiss dude. Stephane wasn't particularly striking physically—he was pale and plain faced with thinning hair, like so many of the other Europeans in that scene. Appearance aside, Stephane had three things going for him: he was tall, he spoke English, and he was flirting with me. No comments on my standards, thank you.

One thing led to another and he walked me back to my little rented studio apartment, where I invited him up. Another thing led to another thing and we were soon groping and grinding. He guided me to the couch, lifted up my leg at the ankle, and put my foot in his mouth. Well, not the whole foot, just my toes.

Because this had never happened to me before, I was kind of shocked and mildly repulsed. *I was just wearing sandals on the streets of Paris! My toes are dusty! What if my feet smell?*

I tried to redirect our erotic activities elsewhere, but he clearly was not as, uh, stimulated as he was with the footplay. I mean, it kinda tickled and wasn't *that* weird, so I just went with it.

The night's activity came to its inevitable climax. Before Stephane melted back into the Parisian streets, we shared a quick goodbye kiss. I kept my lips pursed, as I hadn't anticipated possibly tasting my own feet, and I didn't really want to try it.

À chacun son goût. To each his own!

TWELVE

Cuba
A Blessing, An Inheritance

Another lifetime ago, I was in a *90 Day Fiancé* type situation, although my situationship was decades before that popular reality series aired. Since marriage equality wasn't yet legal in either country, ours was a long distance relationship across borders and a very contentious U.S. economic embargo. Nevertheless, like Gladys Knight and the Pips sang, love finds its own way.

Félix and I only spent twenty or so days together in person, the first time on a starry-eyed whirlwind of a long weekend in his home city of Havana. Smitten, months later I returned for a two-week course at the University of Havana, a "cultural exchange" approved for participation by U.S. residents.

But my real purpose in that visit was to spend time with this handsome suave AfroLatino three years younger than me, cocoa skinned and wavy black haired, who wrote syrupy sweet letters and emails shaping our coupledom into existence. Of course, I was a willing and eager mate and sugar daddy—or "Papi Riki" in local slang. Western Union was our friend.

It wasn't all transactional, though. Felix was a proud cultural broker and quasi tour guide. One bright afternoon, we headed through the Habana Vieja neighborhood to the local ferry terminal, where he paid a minimal fare and we boarded a rickety passenger boat. I was a little concerned about safety, but like many things in Havana, the boat was old but still crankin'. Plus, I figured I could doggie paddle back to shore if sink or swim became the only options. Fortunately none of that came to pass, as the ferry ride across Havana Bay was brief and pleasant, the sea breeze bringing cool relief to the journey.

We disembarked in the suburban town of Regla, and walked through the calm but unremarkable village streets en route to the destination of our pilgrimage, the Iglesia de Nuestra Señora de Regla (Church of Our Lady of Regla).

Inside the colonial structure, modest by Catholic standards, stood an ornate golden altar in which a glowing figurine of the Virgen de Regla, the holy Mother, was perched. Shrouded in her signature baby blues, this Black Madonna is revered as the patron saint of sailors, an important icon for a bayside community like Regla, where seafarers would seek her blessing before launching on their watery journeys. Of greater significance to me was her dual identity as

Yemanya, the Yoruba-derived mother deity of the sea, donned in ocean blue robes.

As with other Yoruba orishas and Catholic saints, La Virgen de Regla / Yemanya was a mashup of spiritual systems brought to the Americas via the Transatlantic slave trade, where this fusion resulted in Brazilian Candomblé, Haitian Voudou, and Santería in Cuba. These spiritual practices and communities provide a strong and direct link to their West African origins, and are a significant part of the national cultural heritage.

Plus, Félix told me, taking my hand in his, La Virgen de Regla / Yemanya is also the protective mother of the gays. I could roll with that; we needed all the support we could get, being queer in a culture that revered full-chested machismo, and Black in a nation that glorified its white Spanish roots.

As Abbey Lincoln, a favorite jazz vocalist and lyricist, once asked in a poem, "Where are the African gods?"

This introduction to African cosmology—whether or not I practice it—made me feel empowered, like interpretations of the divine reflect us, too. And armed with that knowledge, I could swim a mile through choppy waters on the strength of self-love.

THIRTEEN

Vietnam
Crafting a New Story

As a child of the Cold War, I grew up associating Vietnam with a vocabulary of trauma: Agent Orange, napalm, *Rambo*, "boat people," and the invisible and vicious Viet Cong. Images of destruction, violence, torture, and oppression seemed on a continuous loop through movies, television, and story lines from the late Senator John McCain to the everyday Vietnam vet.

As an adult visitor, I first disembarked in Vietnam at Ha Long Bay, a beautiful UNESCO World Heritage site in the Gulf of Tonkin. Fog sat over the bay waters, peaceful and patient. Our small boat navigated closer to the rounded mounds of island rock jutting skyward from the sea, drawing us closer to gaze at their stone formations and tree-dotted shores. Everything was so serene, in direct contrast to the ominous narrative I'd grown up absorbing.

Another counterpoint appeared while our tour group biked through the countryside of Da Nang, riding by a photoshoot of a betrothed couple—him in a crisp white shirt, small black bowtie, and tuxedo pants; her in a stylish beige *áo dài*, the national dress of Vietnam, with a fitted waist and slit on either side of the leg. Despite each of them moving with care to remain balanced inside the slender canoes that sat in riverside reeds, they looked so happy and taken with one another, joking with friends assisting with the photoshoot. We wished them well as we continued our two-wheeled journey.

Further affirmation came through the optimistic voices of three students who approached me in Ho Chi Minh City wanting to practice their already quite good English. They shared how proud they were to be Vietnamese in this day and age, expressing a sense of excitement about their futures.

The students indulged my request for a photo in front of the long-bearded statue of the city's namesake, their national founding father. As the camera snapped, one student flashed a peace sign, one gave a thumbs up, and one smiled while rocking an OBEY hoodie, the brand birthed from the U.S. street art and skateboarding scene. The Western influences were not lost on me; neither was their sincere-seeming patriotism.

A camo-covered U.S. fighter jet greeted visitors to the War Remnants Museum, formerly known as the "Museum of War Crimes." The exhibitions were shocking—some of them outright propaganda, evoking old narratives of aggression, atrocity, and violence.

A U.S. vet in our tour group, when asked for his thoughts about what he'd just seen in the museum, told us "There are different ways of telling the truth. You just had to be there."

He fell silent after that. Tears filled his eyes.

The ripple effects of the War, which ended in 1975, may be diminishing in the American imagination as Vietnam vets move through seniorhood, and relations between the U.S. and Vietnam settle into their third decade of normalization. I am not naive enough to think that trauma leaves behind no scars, but perhaps those few days in Vietnam revealed a healing that comes from the passage of years. A softening of hard lines as flowers blossom where there was once only mud.

FOURTEEN

South Africa & Singapore
Something Bold, Something New

One of the joys of traveling is sampling the delicacies and staples of a given location, then either incorporating these new tastes into one's own life where possible–like eating sardines or churros–or leaving the tasting as an adventure and a memory, no diss to the home culture. I present two nominees for the latter category:

On my final night in Johannesburg during my first

trip there, I connected with a friend and neighbor from Oakland who was also in town. He invited me to a swanky restaurant in Sandton, an upscale suburb of Joburg, complete with sleek glass and steel office buildings and retail experiences to match.

A popular menu item was mopane worms, the finger-sized caterpillar larvae of the emperor moth. Named after the tree in which they live, mopane worms are recognized as an abundant source of protein. They're gutted, boiled, and then deep-fried with garlic and tomato. When introducing something new and perhaps strange to my palate, I try my best not to frown, scowl, or allow a dramatic pause before diving in, especially if hosts from that home country are watching. "It tastes a little like chicken," so the joke goes, perhaps to prepare one's taste buds or to stir up a little comestible courage. We should know better by now–even chicken tastes different from place to place!

The dish of warm mopane worms, stacked like Lincoln Logs, arrived at our table. I speared one with a fork. It was kind of crispy and kind of chewy, "like a vegan sausage link," I later wrote in my notes. Saw it. Did it. The End.

In other culinary adventures, a Filipino colleague had both warned and encouraged me about tasting durian, a large pod fruit grown and consumed in Southeast Asia. Durian looks like one of those spiky shell backpacks that were in vogue in the 2010s. The fruit is notorious for its stinky odor, which is both the appeal and the challenge of eating the soft yellow flesh inside the pod. Durians are so malodorous that they're banned by name in Singapore's spotless public transportation system, with signs posted throughout the stations and trains: No smoking, no eating or drinking, no flammable goods, and NO DURIANS.

The cafe in my Singapore hotel featured a display case of treats all made with durian. The assorted pastries and puddings were lovely to look at, and made my mouth water, as a big fan of lemon desserts.

Trying to eat one was a different story. I chose a durian eclair. The texture was silky like a custard, but I couldn't get an accurate sense of the taste because the stench was so strong. Imagine sniffing the bottom of a public garbage bin outdoors on a hot day. Yeah, that kind of stink. I had to brush twice with a disposable toothbrush and gargle mint mouthwash before I was allowed within kissing distance of Hubby. Nasty smell.

But given the chance, I might try either of these items again. Maybe the prep would be different; maybe my palate has changed. I remain open to the spirit of adventure–within reason.

In Hong Kong, I flat out refused to try the duck tongues, fanned out in a fancy circle on the serving plate like little scarlet strawberry wedges. I stuck with vegetarian options that evening, thank you very much.

FIFTEEN

Germany
Wide Open Space

I have a long-standing interest in public spaces for recreation and reflection, and the repurposing of old structures for new uses in clever ways. New York's High Line project is a great example, having transformed a disused elevated railway into a gorgeous winding garden and sculpture park. This explains why I was so intrigued by Tempelhofer Feld, a former airfield turned recreational park, now the largest urban open space in the world. I saw a video clip about it on a travel show, and when I had an opportunity to visit Berlin for the first time, Tempelhofer was on my list of must-sees.

Germany was not a destination that was on my priority list, but once I found myself there for business, I realized what an unexpected impact twentieth century German history has had on me. Stories of the Third Reich's persecution of Jews and others haunted me as a young boy after I watched the four-day TV miniseries *Holocaust*. I lay awake in bed freaked out by the atrocities, making the connection to my own nation's history of racial violence: "Will that ever happen to us??"

In the sixth grade I completed a scrapbooked report on East Germany, complete with a cover drawing of the old communist emblem, a compass and hammer surrounded by a wreath of rye. For the report, I wrote to the East German embassy in Washington D.C. I recall that the manila envelope of information they sent to me arrived in the U.S. mail already opened. [Cue ominous music here.]

For me as an '80s sports enthusiast, East Germans were second string boogeymen to our American athletes–only the Soviets were more loathed. Their state-sponsored athletic training produced stellar results, some of which we now know were driven by doping practices and unethical experimentation.

So I already had a bit of context and historical familiarity with Germany, although not the best impressions. But what better remedy than travel to update and alter perceptions?

Tempelhofer Feld is a huge oval of grass in south central Berlin, crossed by two asphalt runways. On the northern perimeter is the former Tempelhof terminal, a massive airport structure built by the German bad guys in between their quests for world domination. When the fallen capital city was divided into quadrants in 1945 by the Allied victors, Tempelhof became a crucial asset for West Berlin. Tempelhof Feld was the drop-off point for the Berlin airlift, which saved the isolated land isle of West Berliners from starvation, as their road and rail entries had been cut off by a communist blockade. After the fall of the Iron Curtain, the airport's commercial operations continued until 2008, when Tempelhofer closed to air traffic and the conversion to a park began.

I rode the clean and efficient Metro to a station at the southwestern corner of Tempelhofer Feld. Equipped with a brilliant raspberry donut and bottle of water, I began a slow walk across the huge field. That day the Feld welcomed all-comers, as Berliners and visitors turned out to enjoy the nascent spring weather. Pleasant crowds roller skated and roller bladed, rode bicycles, flew kites, lounged on the grass, or sauntered while savoring a donut.

I was most intrigued by the huge runway. I felt like a Lilliputian, walking along the center stripes, taking in the views on either side of me, including a cordoned off Skylark Protection Zone, the mating grounds for the endangered native birds.

I reached the far park exit in a little over thirty minutes, feet aching from significant walking from throughout the day. Just by being there, enjoying the laid-back, peaceful energy, I felt that I belonged in this larger urban community—precisely the sense such spaces are meant to evoke.

Auch ich bin ein Berliner.

SIXTEEN

Panama
A Man, A Plan, a Canal

Once upon a time, I decided to focus on improving my grasp of spoken Spanish. Despite years of primary school through college instruction, as well as day-to-day opportunities while living in California, my comprehension and conversation skills were still limited and disappointing. I figured that a language immersion program would force me, maybe stumbling and bumbling, toward greater proficiency.

Que Dios me bendiga.

A colleague had previously raved about her visit to Panama, particularly her time in the rainforest, sharing that the ecotourism was as good as world-renowned Costa Rica but less popular. Geography buff that I am, I was also drawn to the opportunity to see the Panama Canal, the twentieth century engineering marvel that it is.

I was also interested in Panama as a Caribbean nation, having befriended two gregarious Black gay men, both Panameño by origin and New Yorker by upbringing, the descendants of West Indian workers who migrated to the canal construction zone to engage in the backbreaking labor. There those forefathers also forged an Afro Caribbean community, largely centered in the Atlantic coastal city of Colón.

I didn't make it to Colón, but my experience in the capital, Panama City, revealed an impressive, bustling metropolis; super ritzy in some places, historic in others, and destitute in a few bleak pockets.

I enrolled in a week-long immersion school where I received four hours of individualized instruction each day. I also completed written assignments each evening. The instructors were patient, friendly, and skillful as teachers and coaches, given that one-on-one learning can be intimidating when conducted in another language. I responded well to the lessons–or maybe it was the attention–and retained an impressive stockpile of vocabulary, extra motivated by having to pay *muchas Balboas*–equal to the U.S. dollar–out of my own pocket.

Aside from figuring out the homework, in my small amount of free time I tooled around the city and environs. At a beach adjacent to the city, I was most intrigued by the sight of massive cargo ships anchored in the Pacific, awaiting their turn to move through the Canal. In one sighting I counted twenty-five moored ships, but learned that the average is sometimes three times that many!

Later, while standing on a balcony at the Miraflores Visitor's Center, a twenty-minute drive from downtown Panama City, I watched as a giant vessel began to pass through the open doors of the closest lock. A microphoned guide narrated the real time action unfolding in front of the small crowd of curious onlookers like me. The Canal serves to "lift" the boats through the varying levels of elevation across the Canal zone, with three locks—Gatun, Pedro Miguel, and Miraflores—serving as aquatic "elevators" to raise or lower the boats depending on the direction which they are passing (Pacific to Atlantic or vice versa). Even though this is the narrowest strip of land between the two oceans, the entire journey takes about ten hours to cross the eighty-two kilometer length of the Canal. That's a speed of about four miles per hour. The doors of the lock, as tall as a seven-story building, open to accommodate the ships, close behind them, fill with water levels on par with the next segment of the journey, and open to allow the ship to pass forward.

After the Canal became fully operative, shipping companies began to build supersized ships, nicknamed Panamax, to maximize the amount of cargo they could carry while still able to squeeze through the canal. Some of the vessels pass with less than ten feet of clearance on either side—and these locks are 110 feet wide! It was fascinating to watch, and the ships' crews were close enough to see their smiling faces as they waved to those of us ashore.

In the years since my visit, I've learned that climate change stands to wreak havoc with the Canal's efficiency, as a severe drought has significantly lowered water levels. This drop in the freshwater that enables ships to pass through locks now threatens to ground the vessels, making the navigation even more perilous.

The Canal's original construction stands as a testament to overcoming daunting challenges. Climate change presents yet another opportunity to test human ingenuity and resolve. May we rise to the occasion.

SEVENTEEN

Ireland
Home Away from Home

My beloved late mother-in-law, Ma Betty, hailed from a big small town in southwest Ireland's County Cork. Small in that there are fewer than 5,000 residents, but bigger still than most of its neighboring towns in the vicinity. Big enough such that others from surrounding rural areas travel into the town center to shop at the stores and restaurants along the two dense main thoroughfares.

Before traveling to County Cork for the first time, Hubby warned me that I might find the accommodations to be spartan. We were scheduled to stay as guests with a cousin's family just down the road from the farm and small stone house where Ma Betty was born.

We flew into Shannon on Ireland's western coast, one of three international airports in the Republic. After a three-hour drive through curvy two-laned roads linking small town to small town, we arrived at our destination, groggy and hungry.

Our hosts were ready for us, having prepared a plentiful "Welcome to Ireland" meal, including the tastiest cabbage outside of my grandmother's kitchen, creamy fresh mashed potatoes, and a light buttery whitefish. Just delightful.

After dinner and conversation, our hosts led us to our accommodations, a small in-law apartment built over the garage. When we opened the door, we discovered our modest expectations were unfounded—the place was decked out like the "after" results of an HGTV home makeover: a sleek leather couch, thirty-inch flatscreen, tiny boutique appliances, French coffee press, locally popular brown bread and black tea on the counter, a slick Scandinavian sunroof, plush down duvet, matching thick bathrobes, and local postcards in the nightstand drawers. The Celtic Tiger had indeed stopped through town!

During our week-long stay, we visited numerous other relatives and were always welcomed with great warmth. One visit stood out. We were invited to the childhood home of four adult sisters, set on a sheep farm in the deep countryside. And I mean *deep*. One of the sisters had to meet us in the nearest village and instructed us to follow her car over the moss green hills, through the woods, and past quiet pastoral scenes right out of a watercolor painting. This place was in the *sticks*.

I wondered deep down how I, likely the most melanated creature around for miles, would be welcomed. On top of that, we were an interracial queer couple, a rare duo in these sparsely populated parts of the Republic. Yet we were regaled, toasted for our still-newish marriage, and treated to a feast: a Thanksgiving-worthy spread of meat and fowl, a cornucopia of vegetables, fresh breads, baked treats, starter soup, jarred sides, and a buffet of desserts. The effect was not showy, but genuine, hearty hospitality in this cozy homestead surrounded by pastures.

We all laughed with gusto, sharing curiosities and family updates, browsing through old photos, recounting memories and stories. At times I struggled to understand some of the verbal exchanges because of how fast they spoke and the pronunciation differences—accented to my ears, normal to theirs. But they were gracious enough to slow and repeat when needed, without talking down to me.

I came to realize that the infamous Irish "brogue" is really nothing more than a strong accent rather than a distinct dialect like a pidgin language.

Our afternoon in the countryside made me very grateful both for family love and for the kindness of strangers–made not so strange through their generosity–in this remote-yet-connected corner of the world. I felt right at home.

THE END

SPECIAL ACKNOWLEDGEMENTS

Many thanks to Joe Sadusky
for on-point feedback
consistent encouragement
and the inspiration of his writing pursuits

AND

To all the friends (and exes)
mentioned but unnamed in these stories
a loving thanks for our adventures together
at home and abroad

ABOUT THE AUTHOR

CEDRIC BROWN is the author of *Eyes of Water & Stone: From Havana with Love*, *Tar Heel Born: A Native Son Speaks on Race, Religion, & Reconciliation*, and *You Are Everything: 10 Starter Stories*. His work is also included in the anthologies *Blacktino Queer Performance* and *The Road Before Us: 100 Black Gay Poets*. Cedric is the founder of the Jacobs/Jones African American Literary Prize, sponsored by the North Carolina Writers Network, and co-founder of the Randall Kenan Prize for Black LGBTQ Fiction, sponsored by Lambda Literary Foundation. He lives in Winston-Salem, North Carolina, USA.

P.O. Box 17506
Winston-Salem, NC 27116
USA

junies.mood@pobox.com

www.ingramcontent.com/pod-product-compliance
Lightning Source LLC
Chambersburg PA
CBHW051954290426
44110CB00015B/2240